I AM
Affirmations of Faith to the New You!

Barbara A. Walker

Copyright © 2013
Barbara A. Walker
All Rights Reserved

Unless otherwise noted, all Scripture quotations are from the New King James Version of the Bible.

For more information or to order additional books, please submit $17.95 (this includes the cost of postage) to:

Barbara A. Walker
377 North Commerce Street
Aurora, Illinois 60504
godswomenofexcellence@gmail.com

Published by Barbara A. Walker

Printed in the USA by
CreateSpace
4900 LaCross Road
North Charleston, SC 29406
USA

DEDICATIONS

This book is dedicated to the best family I could have ever had. I am blessed to be loved by so many. *"We started from the bottom, now we here!"*, in the place that the Lord God ordained for us to be. All praises to the most-high God for so richly blessing us.

In loving memory to my mom, Pearlie Mae Lee Jackson, who was the wind beneath my wings and my biggest cheerleader, always saying , "you **can** do it!" (no matter what **IT** was), and my brother, Hardis Lee Jackson, Jr. (JR).

To my dad, Mr. Hardis Lee Jackson, Sr., and my cool siblings: Jennifer, Cedric, Kimberly, Gewanda, Valerie, Martin, Tracey, and Michael.

To God's greatest gift to me in my beautiful children: Antonio, Bernadette, Eric, and Shamica, and the most fantabulous grandchildren *ever:* Devonte, Trestin, TaeShaun, Aniya, Tyler, and Anthony, Jr.

The Lord our God is an awesome God. I want to thank and praise Him for all of His wondrous blessings upon my life!

My Declaration of Praise

1: I will bless the Lord at all times; His praise shall continually be in my mouth.
2: My soul shall make its boast in the Lord; the humble shall hear of it and be glad.
3: Oh, magnify the Lord with me, and let us exalt His name together.
8: Oh, taste and see that the Lord is good; blessed is the man who trusts in Him!
Psalm 34

Preface

We wake up each day with the opportunity to make choices. Will I face this day with joy or discontent? Will I thank God for my blessings or complain about the unfairness of life? Will I seek opportunity to do good or look only for what I can get? Will I see myself as God sees me or will I allow the world's opinions and ideals to shape my vision of who I AM? You know – choices.

God is an amazing God. He looked out over this world that He created and declared that "it is good". He had created perfection, and He was proud of His creation. He had made everything ready – the land, the air, the creatures, the plant life, and the atmosphere – so that it was prepared for the man who would be created in "His image and His likeness".

So, we fast-forward to Israel, God's chosen people, being delivered from Egyptian slavery. God called the man Moses to be His voice and leader during this time. Moses had many objections. Finally, he asked God (in essence), "Who are You? When I go back to Egypt and tell them that You have sent me to deliver them, they will want to know Your name; they will want to know on whose authority I have come." God said, "I AM WHO I AM." And He said, "Thus you shall say to the children of Israel, 'I AM has sent me to you.'" (Exodus 3:14).

Every time I read that, I think "wow!" What an awesome God we serve that He could identify Himself simply and sufficiently as "I AM"! Self-sufficient. Sovereign. Supreme. Self-existent. Sacred.

Exodus 3:14 is one of the most famous verses in the Torah. Hayah means "existed" or "was" in Hebrew; "ehyeh" is the first person singular imperfect form and is usually translated in English Bibles as "I will be" (or "I shall be"), for example, at Exodus 3:12. Ehyeh asher ehyeh literally translates as "I Will Be What I Will Be", with attendant theological and mystical implications in Jewish tradition. However, in most English Bibles, this phrase is rendered as "I am that I am."

The God of the Bible, the Creator of the universe with a special relationship to mankind, first reveals Himself to a whole people group in the book of Exodus, just before He rescues them from captivity in Egypt. He reveals himself to Moses and appoints him as His prophet. He reveals himself as "I AM WHO I AM", the One whose being needs no other explanation, the One who has always existed, the One known by Moses' ancestors, the One is everything Moses and his people need.

In ancient Hebrew, the name "I AM" was probably pronounced as "Yahweh", and may be translated in our Bible as "the LORD". The precise pronunciation is not really important. What matters is who He is, and what that means to us. He appears to Moses in a fiery manifestation, and speaks the following words, though His actual being remains hidden.[1]

Ehyeh-Asher-Ehyeh (often contracted in English as "I AM") is one of the Seven Names of God accorded special care by medieval

---

[1] http://jesusisreal.org/I_AM.htm

Jewish tradition.[2] It was the name by which God identified Himself to Moses, and it was the name by which Jesus identified Himself to the Jews. When questioned, Jesus boldly declared, "Your father Abraham rejoiced at the thought of seeing my day; he saw it and was glad." "You are not yet fifty years old," the Jews said to Him, "and you have seen Abraham!" "I tell you the truth," Jesus answered, "before Abraham was born, I AM (Yahweh)!" (John 8:56 – 58). Jesus' response made them so angry that they wanted to stone Him because they recognized that He was identifying Himself as God.

Our God – the only wise God, the God who was, who is, and who is to come. We are not God, nor are we equal with God. But we are the children of God, created in "His image and His likeness". We cannot identify ourselves as I AM, but we can make some bold declarations of who we are in Him. Recognizing and realizing our reality in Him can change our outlook on our entire lives! It can refocus us, reenergize us, reengage us, and help us to renew our minds. I am a child of the King – who are you?

We will explore some "I Am" statements together. Don't be surprised if Satan comes against you to create doubt about the truth of these statements. If he can keep you uninformed and ignorant of who you are in Christ, he can keep your focus off your fulfilling your purpose and walking into your destiny.

---

[2] The Reader's Encyclopedia, Second Edition 1965, publisher Thomas Y. Crowell Co., New York, editions 1948, 1955. Library of Congress Catalog Card No. 65-12510, page 918

Don't listen to him! Believe God and all that He says about you. These are declarations of our faith. They are announcements of our identities. They are affirmations of our positions in the Kingdom of God. They are testimonies of our complete trust in our Father. They are our pronouncements to help each of us better understand just who we are in Christ, recognizing that they are our avowals of agreement with God that we are complete in Him, "*... vessel(s) for honor, sanctified and useful for the Master, prepared for every good work.*" (II Timothy 2:21)

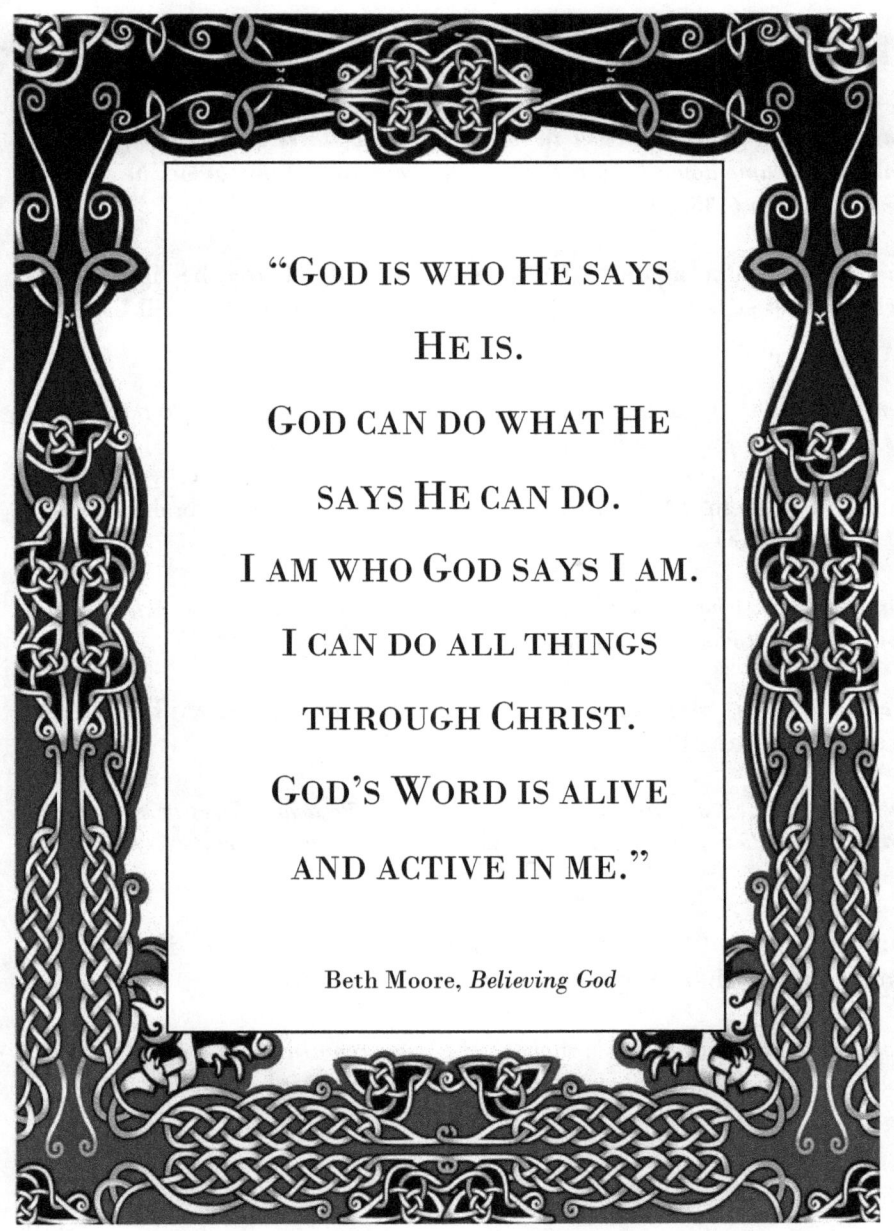

"God is who He says He is.
God can do what He says He can do.
I am who God says I am.
I can do all things through Christ.
God's Word is alive and active in me."

Beth Moore, *Believing God*

The "I AM" Statements of Jesus the Christ

Then Jesus declared, "I am the bread of life. He who comes to me will never go hungry, and he who believes in me will never be thirsty." "I am the living bread which came down from heaven. If anyone eats of this bread, he will live forever;" (John 6:35, 51)

When Jesus spoke again to the people, he said, "I am the light of the world. Whoever follows me will never walk in darkness, but will have the light of life." (John 8:12)

Therefore I said to you that you will die in your sins; for if you do not believe that I am He, you will die in your sins."

Jesus said to them, "Most assuredly, I say to you, before Abraham was, I AM." (John 8:58)

"I am the gate; whoever enters through me will be saved. He will come in and go out, and find pasture." (John 10:9)

"I am the Good Shepherd. The Good Shepherd lays down His life for the sheep." (John 10:11)

Jesus said to her, "I am the resurrection and the life. He who believes in me will live, even though he dies; and whoever lives and believes in me will never die." (John 11:25-26)

Jesus answered, "I am the way and the truth and the life. No one comes to the Father except through me." (John 14:6)

"I am the vine; you are the branches. If a man remains in me and I in him, he will bear much fruit; apart from me you can do nothing." (John 15:5)

"I AM!"

I AM[3]

Eddie James

I am the Lord, I'm the almighty God
I am the one for whom nothing is too hard
I am the Shepherd and I am the door
I am the good news to the bound and the poor

I am the righteous one and I am the Lamb
I am the ram in the bush for Abraham
I am the ultimate sacrifice for sin
I am your Redeemer, the beginning and the end

I am Jehovah and I am the King
I am the Messiah, David's offspring
I am your high priest and I am the Christ
I am the resurrection, I am the light

I am the bread and I am the wine
I am your future, so leave your past behind
I am the one in the midst of two or three
I am your tabernacle, I am your jubilee

I am hope, I am peace, I am joy, I am rest
I am your comfort and relief from your stress
I am strength, I am faith, I am love, I am power
I am your freedom this very hour!

---

[3] http://www.youtube.com/watch?v=JAX7TXvQZ0U

INTRODUCTION

I heard a powerful testimony during a worship experience. A young lady told us how the Lord had delivered her from low self-esteem and depression. She said she had struggled with suicidal thoughts for years, and had attempted it twice. But she declared to us that day that she has been set free! She thought that no one loved her, and she didn't love herself. But as Michael Jackson said, "That was then, this is now!" Because of the blood of Jesus, she could boldly say "I Am!" [4]

She said she had come to the realization that she is beautiful. She realized that she is loved and valued for who she is. The devil didn't want her to know that. As long as she thought so little of herself that she wanted to die, he knew he had her bound. But when she came to know the truth – that God loves her because she is lovable – she was set free. And her testimony provided deliverance for many others in the house who were struggling with their own fears and doubts of who they are.

We are not who others say we are. But we are all that God says we are. Too many times, we allow people to get into our heads, and we start living out what they say about us. We believe we're ugly if someone calls us that. We allow ourselves to fail because someone says that we will. We call ourselves sick based on the doctor's diagnosis.

But, let's flip that script and start saying what God says about us! We cannot be ugly because we were "created in His image and His

---

[4] Reprint from Barbara A. Walker, W.O.E. Word, godswomenofexcellence, August 6, 2013.

likeness", and God says "we are fearfully and wonderfully made". No way can we fail because "we can do all things through Christ who gives us strength" and we are "more than conquerors". Regardless of what the doctor says, we are healed "by His stripes".

It's time to turn the devil on his head. God has blessed us, share it. His favor is upon us, reveal it. The joy of the Lord is our strength, shout it. Say out loud your "I AM" declarations so that the devil can hear them, but more importantly, so that you can hear them. Because you have to believe that you are who Gods says you are, you can do what God says you can do, and you have what God says you can have. God is faithful, and we have His Word on it. Believe it. Live it.

That is my prayer for each of you, my sisters. I pray for your strength. I pray for your peace. I pray for your joy. And I pray that God will allow you to see that you are all that He has created you to be. Stop listening to the lies of the enemy; see yourself as God sees you. Say it aloud. Hear yourself say about you what God says about you: I AM victorious. I AM faithful. I AM a believer. I AM healed. I AM redeemed. I AM rejoicing. I AM holy. I AM righteous. I AM free! God does not see us as we were or even as we are; God sees us as we will be. And that, my sister, is perfect and whole, with nothing missing and nothing broken, because we will become just as He is. That is the picture of a glorious new you. That is the reality of realizing that in Christ, "I AM"!

14: I will praise You, for I am fearfully and wonderfully made; marvelous are Your works, and that my soul knows very well. (Psalm 139)

18: But we all, with unveiled face, beholding as in a mirror the glory of the Lord, are being transformed into the same image from glory to glory, just as by the Spirit of the Lord.[5]

1: Behold what manner of love the Father has bestowed on us, that we should be called children of God! Therefore the world does not know us, because it did not know Him.
2: Beloved, now we are children of God; and it has not yet been revealed what we shall be, but we know that when He is revealed, we shall be like Him, for we shall see Him as He is.
3: And everyone who has this hope in Him purifies himself, just as He is pure.[6]

Father, thank You for creating us in Your image and in Your likeness. We know that Satan wants to keep us bound in fear and doubt. Help us to see ourselves as You see us, victorious, healthy, sane, redeemed, whole, holy, righteous, joyful, and free. You have already given us everything that we need to live fulfilled lives here in the earth even as we prepare for our lives to come. Thank You for making it so. In Jesus' name. Amen.

SELAH ~~ THINK ON THIS!
"BELIEVE IN YOURSELF AND THERE WILL COME A DAY WHEN OTHERS WILL HAVE NO CHOICE BUT TO BELIEVE WITH YOU."
(Cynthia Kersey)

"ACCEPT WHO YOU ARE AND REVEL IN IT."
(Mitch Albom)

---

[5] II Corinthians 3
[6] I John 3

"One Day My Soul Just Opened Up"[7]

One day my soul just opened up
    and things started happenin'
    things I can't quite explain
    I mean
    I cried and cried like never before
    I cried tears of then thousand mothers
    I couldn't even feel anything because
    I cried 'til I was numb.

One day my soul just opened up
    I felt this overwhelming pride
    what I was proud of
    only God knows!
    Like the pride of a hundred thousand fathers
    basking in the glory of their newborn sons
    I was grinnin' from ear to ear!

One day my soul just opened up
    I started laughing
    and I laughed for what seemed like forever
    wasn't nothin' particularly funny goin' on
    but I laughed anyhow
    I laughed the joy of a million children playin'
    in the mud
    I laughed 'til my sides ached
    Oh God! It felt so good!

---

[7] Vanzant, Iyanla. *"One Day My Soul Just Opened Up"*. Poem written by Gemmia L. Vanzant.

One day my soul just opened up

    There were revelations, annihilations, and resolutions
    feelings of doubt and betrayal, vengeance and forgiveness
    memories of things I'd seen and done before
    of places I'd been, although I didn't know when
    there were lives I'd lived
    people I'd loved
    battles I'd fought
    victories I'd won
    and wars I'd lost

One day, my soul just opened up
    And out poured all the things
    I'd been hiding
    and denying
    and living through
    that had just happened moments before

One day, my soul just opened up
    and I decided
    I was good and ready!
    I was good and ready
    to surrender
    my life
    to God.

So, with my soul wide open,
    I sat down
    wrote Him a note
    and told Him so.

I've been reading these devotionals for several years now, and they have always been right on time. However, today's devotional really hit home with me today. Thank you for allowing the Spirit of God direct you in your writings. I don't know how much feedback you get from these devotionals, so I wanted to let you know that they are blessing me.

I've been trying to write a daily devotional book for a couple of years now, your consistency has convicted and challenged me. You have never missed a single day, and here I am making excuses as to why I can only write once or twice a week, many times not even that often. You have really encouraged me throughout the years, and now I have no excuse.

I am quite sure that I am not the only person that has been richly blessed by your ministry. Thank you again for what you do. Many blessings to you.
Quincy S., Indianapolis

Just like moons and like suns,
With the certainty of tides,
Just like hopes springing high,
Still I'll rise.[8]

---

[8] Excerpted from the poem *"Still I Rise"* by Maya Angelou

I AM
Able

~~ *having necessary power, skill, resources,*
or qualifications; qualified ~~

"I can do all things through Christ who strengthens me."
Philippians 4:13

"Now to Him who is able to do exceedingly abundantly
above all that we ask or think, according to
the power that works in us,"
Ephesians 3:20

I AM
Accepted

~~ *generally approved; usually regarded as normal, right* ~~

"…to the praise of the glory of His grace, by which He made us
accepted in the Beloved."
Ephesians 1:6

It is fitting that we begin renewing our minds by acknowledging that we are **able** and **accepted** as our first I AM statements. Fear causes us to doubt ourselves in so many ways. It makes us afraid to try, and if we try, we fear that we will be rejected as not good enough or strong enough or pretty enough or able enough. But we are able to do all with Christ, because the Word of God tells us that we can! We don't need the acceptance of others when we have His Word that we have been accepted in the beloved.

What does that look like? You may be asking, "How do I learn to trust God for everything?" "How do I know that I am following God and not my own desires?" it is a wonderful state of privilege to be *"accepted in the Beloved"*! It includes our justification before God, but in the Greek, the term "acceptance" means more than that.[9] It signifies that we are the objects of divine complacence, even of

---

[9] Bible Gateway. Charles Spurgeon's Morning and Evening, September 23, 2013.

divine delight. How marvelous that it is to know that we are the objects of divine love! But it is only "in the Beloved".

Some Christians seem to be accepted in their own experience; at least, that is their apprehension. When their spirit is lively, and their hopes bright, they think God accepts them, for they feel so high, so heavenly-minded, so drawn above the earth! But when their souls cleave to the dust, they are the victims of the fear that they are no longer accepted. If they could only see that all their high joys do not exalt them, and all their low despondencies do not really depress them in the Father's sight, but that they stand accepted in One who never alters, in One who is always the beloved of God, always perfect, always without spot or wrinkle, or any such thing, how much happier they would be, and how much more they would honor the Savior! Rejoice then, believer, in this: you are accepted "in the beloved".

Our assurance of this can be found in the Word of God. Know for sure that the Spirit of the living God will never lead us in any way which is contrary to His Word. If my desire causes me to transgress or sin against God, then I can know with a certainty that it is not of God. If my feelings of acceptance are in doubt, then I can know with a certainty that it is not of God. Satan whispers lies in our ears, trying to make us doubt the love that God has for us.

Decide today – on purpose – to trust the Lord for everything. Before speaking. Before acting. Before ... ask God to direct your path and order your step. Before ... seek the Lord's guidance. Then we can be assured of success. Joshua 1:8 tells us: *"This Book of the Law shall not depart from your mouth, but you shall meditate in it day and night, that you may observe to do according to all that is written in it. For then you will make your way prosperous, and then you will have good success."* And be confident that we have been accepted in the beloved, regardless of what others may say.

Prayer of Affirmation ~~
Father, I thank You that I am able to do all things in Christ and I am accepted in You. You cannot fail, and because I am Your daughter, neither can I. You have equipped me for success. My responsibility is to be obedient to Your Word and the leading of Your Holy Spirit. You have promised that You will make my way prosperous, and I will have good success. Thank You, Lord, that I am able and accepted in the Beloved. In Jesus' name. Amen.

My "I AM" Affirmation:
I AM able and living an abundant life because I have been accepted in the beloved, making me special and secure in Christ.

Today, I will:

- ➢ Seek God for His direction for this day.
- ➢ Believe in my abilities to accomplish my goals.
- ➢ Be content in who I am as one of His daughters who has been accepted in the Beloved.
- ➢ Thank God for enabling me to do all things through Christ who gives me strength.
- ➢ Seek the opportunity to encourage someone else.

My thoughts: _____

_____

_____

_____

I AM
Beautiful

~~ having beauty; possessing qualities that give great pleasure or satisfaction to see, hear, think about, etc. ~~

"I will praise You, for I am fearfully and wonderfully made; Marvelous are Your works,
and that my soul knows very well."
Psalm 139:14

I AM
Blessed

~~ consecrated; sacred; holy; sanctified ~~

"Oh, taste and see that the Lord is good;
blessed is the man who trusts in Him!"
Psalm 34:8

What do you see when you look in the mirror. Do you say a beautiful and blessed daughter of the King? Do you see someone who has been made in the image and likeness of her Father? Do you see the glory of the Lord radiating from You? Do you see Jesus?

You should! Your beauty is not in the shape your body or your skin tone or the length or texture of your hair. It is not an outcome of what society has determined. Rather, real beauty begins in your spirit, invades your soul, and is manifested physically. Your beauty is evidenced by your kindness, your joy, your peace, and your security in knowing that you are blessed.

I Peter 3:3 – 4 reads: *"Do not let your adornment be merely outward – arranging the hair, wearing gold, or putting on fine apparel – rather let it be the hidden person of the heart, with the incorruptible beauty of a gentle and quiet spirit, which is very precious in the sight of God."*

Don't compare yourself to models, actresses, and others that people aspire to look like. Remember, they have paid professionals who help them to look that way. Trust me – they didn't wake up with that face on! Instead, focus on being the best YOU that you can be. Take pride in who God created you to be. Learn to love yourself, and you will know that you are a beautiful and blessed daughter of the King.

Prayer of Affirmation ~~
Father, thank You for creating me in Your image and Your likeness. Because I am Your daughter, I know that I am beautiful and I am abundantly blessed. I will honor You by loving myself in a healthy way and living my life to the fullness so that others will see Your glory through me. Thank You, Lord, that I am beautiful and blessed. In Jesus' name. Amen.

My "I AM" Affirmation:
I AM beautiful because I am blessed to be one of God's daughters.

Today, I will:

- Thank God for blessing me to be His beautiful daughter.
- See myself as God sees me.
- Meditate on Psalm 139:14 as a reminder that "*I am fearfully and wonderfully made*".
- Seek the opportunity to encourage someone else.

My thoughts: _____

_____

_____

I AM
Chosen
~~ *selected from several; preferred* ~~

"For many are called, but few are chosen."
Matthew 22:14

I AM
Confident
~~ *sure of oneself; having no uncertainty about one's own abilities, correctness, successfulness, etc.* ~~

"Being confident of this very thing, that He who
has begun a good work in you will complete it
until the day of Jesus Christ;"
Philippians 1:6

"Let us therefore come boldly to the throne of grace, that we may
obtain mercy and find grace to help in time of need."
Hebrews 4:160

I once heard a story about a young woman who was searching for her birth mother. She was happy. She was fulfilled, but she felt a need to find her birth mother. She loved her adoptive parents with all her heart, but that need would not be filled until she found her birth mother.

After years of searching, she finally found her. She was elated! Over time, they developed a good relationship. But nothing could come between her and the mother who had raised her. When asked about it sometime later by a magazine reporter, she provided a really good answer. She explained that she had been blessed to have chosen by her adoptive mother, which made her feel special. It gave her the confidence to go after her goals and dreams because she knew that she was especially loved, not out of duty, but out of desire.

I think of that often as I consider my relationship with God. He **chose** me, adopted me into His family, and made me an heir and joint-heir with Christ. Not out of duty – He owed me nothing. He did it because He wanted a relationship with me, and He was willing to pay the price to have it. I am a confident woman today because I have the assurance of knowing that God loves me, and He specially chose **me** to be a part of His royal family.

To choose means to "select from a number of possibilities," or to "pick by preference."[10] It should be an honorable feeling to know that you've been preferred by God. Of everyone in the world He could have called to perform a task, He chose YOU! Women in every line of work, with different marital statuses, and in different seasons of life, have been chosen by God. Sacrificing is part of our DNA. You didn't have to choose me, but You did. I'm grateful!

Prayer of Affirmation ~~
Father, thank You for choosing me and giving me the confidence to come boldly before Your throne with everything that affects my life. You chose me – handpicked me out of the mess of my life and called me by name – and for that I give You praise. Thank You, Lord, that I have been chosen by You, which makes me a confident woman in You. In Jesus' name. Amen.

My "I AM" Affirmation:
I AM confident because I have been chosen by God as one of His own.

---

[10] McCollors, Tia. Bible Gateway: *Sisters in Faith*. September 30, 2013

Today, I will:

- ➢ Thank God for choosing me and adopting me into His family.
- ➢ Reflect on the wonderful privilege of being chosen by God.
- ➢ Be confident that I am loved, valued, and have His blessed assurance of abundant life in Him.
- ➢ Seek the opportunity to encourage someone else.

My thoughts: _____

_____

_____

_____

****

> TO FREE US FROM THE EXPECTATIONS OF OTHERS, TO GIVE US BACK TO OURSELVES — THERE LIES THE GREAT, SINGULAR POWER OF SELF-RESPECT.
> Joan Didion

I AM
Delivered

~~ *to carry and turn over to the intended recipient or* recipients ~

"Indeed it was for my own peace that I had great bitterness; but You have lovingly delivered my soul from the pit of corruption, for You have cast all my sins behind Your back."
Isaiah 38:17

When you are going through a dark period in life, nothing gives you more hope than knowing that there is an end in sight. Depression. Alcohol or drugs. An abusive relationship. Financial challenges. Sickness or disease. It doesn't matter what the problem, your prayer is that somehow, you will make it out.

Israel spent 430 years in Egypt, but when God delivered them, He brought them out stronger than when they went in. They went in seventy souls; they came out with an estimated 3.5 million souls strong. They came out healthy. They came out wealthy. He delivered them with His mighty hand.

Today, God is still our deliverer! He has promised that He will never leave us or forsake us. We worry, we fret, we doubt, we want to give up, but God is always there. Just as He was with Israel in Egypt, He is with us in our times of darkness. Trust Him – He **will** deliver.

Prayer of Affirmation ~~
Father, thank You for reminding me that no matter what it looks like, You are there! It is Your strength and Your peace which has sustained me as I went through, and I never want to forget that it was You who brought me out. Whether I am in a valley, just made it through a valley, or on my way into a valley, I want to say "thank You". I know that I could not make it without You by my side. Thank You, Lord,

for delivering me out of every dark place I have been in throughout my life. In Jesus' name. Amen.

My "I AM" Affirmation:
I AM at peace because I have been delivered from the bonds of sin and death into the Kingdom of the living God.

Today, I will:

- ➢ Look up and remember the goodness of the Lord.
- ➢ Refuse to focus on the negative things happening in my life.
- ➢ Thank God for always being with me, in spite of my circumstances.
- ➢ Seek the opportunity to encourage someone else.

My thoughts: _____

_____

_____

I AM
Excellence
~~ *the state, quality, or condition of excelling; superiority* ~~

"Therefore, whether you eat or drink, or whatever you do, do all to
the glory of God."
I Corinthians 10:31

"For we are His workmanship, created in Christ Jesus
for good works, which God prepared beforehand
that we should walk in them."
Ephesians 2:10

Ralph Martson said "Excellence is not a skill. It is an attitude." The more educated and affluent we have become as a nation of people, the more eroded this attitude has become. People used to take pride in things: their appearance, their work, their homes, their families.

The way we dress, the care we take for ourselves, and the reputation we have in our communities are all areas in which we once took a lot of pride but no longer seem to care about. This has seeped into our attitudes toward our children's education, our work ethic, our commitment to the church, our families, how we raise our children, even our relationships with God. Nothing and no one seems to generate a spirit of excellence in people the way it once did.

But we should never forget that our God is a god of excellence. Everything He does is excellent, and He expects us to continually strive for excellence in ourselves. We are His ambassadors, His representatives in the earth, and He wants us to be true representatives of Him while we are here. In order to do that, we must change our thinking. We have to approach everything with an *attitude of excellence* by giving it our all. Never settle. Don't compromise. Refuse to make excuses. Press for excellence in every area of our lives. As you do this on a regular basis, you will find your attitude changing from one of doing "just enough" to one of excellence.

"Excellence can be obtained if you:[11]
    ... care more than others think is wise;
    ... risk more than others think is safe;
    ... dream more than others think is practical;
    ... expect more than others think is possible."

An attitude of excellence sets you apart from the pack. An attitude of excellence separates you from the crowd. An attitude of excellence is one more way you can let your light shine. Having an attitude of anything less than excellence not only sells you short, it dishonors God. He deserves much more than that.

Prayer of Affirmation ~~
Father, thank You for giving me all I need to live a life of excellence. As I do, I know it honors and glorifies You. Let that be my main motivation so that I never stop striving to be the best I can be, regardless of what it is that I am doing. Thank You, Lord, for giving me a spirit of excellence in You. In Jesus' name. Amen.

My "I AM" Affirmation:
I AM a woman of excellence whose standards have been set by God.

Today, I will:

- ➢ Strive for an attitude of excellence.
- ➢ Remind myself that my attitude and my actions reflect upon God.
- ➢ Repent of any shortcomings and determine to make today (and the next) a more excellent day.

---

[11] http://thinkexist.com/quotation/excellence_can_be_obtained_if_you-care_more_than/9638.html

- ➢ Refuse to compromise in order to "fit in".
- ➢ Seek the opportunity to encourage someone else.

My thoughts: _____

_____

_____

_____

~~~~~~~~~~~~~~~~~~~~

The willingness to accept responsibility for one's own life is the source from which self-respect springs.
Joan Didion

I AM
Forgiven

*~~ excused for a fault or an offense; pardon;
to absolve from payment of ~~*

"In Him we have redemption through His blood, the forgiveness of sins, according to the riches of His grace."
Ephesians 1:7

Free

*~~ enjoying personal rights or liberty, as a person
who is not in slavery ~~*

"Therefore if the Son makes you free,
you shall be free indeed."
John 8:38

"Now the Lord is the Spirit; and where the Spirit
of the Lord is, there is liberty."
II Corinthians 3:17

Our freedom in Christ loosens our shackles and breaks the chains of sin which had us bound. Now, we can sing, jump, shout, and praise Him a little louder than before. We are forgiven, and our forgiveness has set us free from the power of sin and the penalty of sin. (Can't you **hear** the chains falling?)

Maybe you never felt bound by your sin? (I pray that's not so.) Because we **were** bound. Inexplicably. Completely. Absolutely. Seemingly irrevocably. Bound in sin which kept us separated us from God. Bound in sin which only reward was death. And like any abnormality or addiction, the very action created within us the desire to continue in it. Intellectually, we knew it was wrong. Yet, we rationalized and tried to justify our actions. We told ourselves that God understood, even as we suffered from the guilt and shame of our sin. But God loved us so much that He gave ...

Through Christ we have been forgiven, setting us completely free from the onus of sin. Since we have been saved, we should no longer walk in fear and condemnation. *"There is therefore now no condemnation to those who are in Christ Jesus, who do not walk according to the flesh, but according to the Spirit. For the law of the Spirit of life in Christ Jesus has made me free from the law of sin and death."*[12]

We are no longer stained by our sin, because we have been covered by the blood of Jesus. Though we may commit sin, we are no longer sinners. You have to believe that! It is the absolute knowing that you are forgiven which makes you free. Jesus took the shame of a sinner's death ~ nailed it to the cross ~ so that we could walk in complete freedom from our sin. You are forgiven!

Prayer of Affirmation ~~
Father, thank You for setting us Your forgiveness of our sins, which has made us free! We have Your assurance that we have been cleansed and made new again in You. Thank You for reminding us that freedom is not just a status, it is also a state of mind. Help us to accept our position in You and all that it provides for us. Thank You, Lord, for forgiving us and making us "free indeed". In Jesus' name. Amen.

My "I AM" Affirmation:
I AM forgiven because I believe in the power of the cross, and I am free because the Spirit of the Lord has made me free indeed.

---

[12] Romans 8:1 – 2

Today, I will:

- ➢ Daily walk in my newness in freedom from sin.
- ➢ Live as one of the forgiven and redeemed of the Lord.
- ➢ Rebuke Satan when he tries to lie to me about my status in the Kingdom.
- ➢ Thank God that He has forgiven me and set me free!
- ➢ Seek the opportunity to encourage someone else.

My thoughts: _____

_____

_____

_____

I AM
Gifted
~~ having great special talent or ability ~~

"But each one has his own gift from God, one in
this manner and another in that."
I Corinthians 7:7

I AM
Generous
~~ liberal in giving or sharing; unselfish ~~

"The generous soul will be made rich, and he who
waters will also be watered himself."
Proverbs 11:25

God has given me gifts! They are special gifts He uniquely designed just for me. He didn't just give me anything which may have been leftover and unused by someone else. He looked at me, considered my S.H.A.P.E.[13], and decided which were the best gifts to fit in with who He created me to be. He gave me gifts which were intended for me and me alone! That thrills me. That excites me. That makes me feel honored. That humbles me. That reminds me of how much I am loved by the great I AM!

My gratitude to Him for His wonderful gifts to me makes want to pay it forward and give back; my gratitude empowers my generous spirit in response to His generosity to me. I want to love more. I want to share my joy. I strive to be a peacemaker. I give more to those in need, all because of all the gifts which God has given me.

---

[13] Warren, Rick. *The Purpose Driven Life.*

Prayer of Affirmation ~~
Father, thank You, for generously giving me gifts. Special gifts of the Spirit – joy, peace, hope, faith. Thank You for giving me gifts of provision. Thank You for giving me gifts of protection. Your gracious generosity of love gives me strength and power. Thank You for gifting me. In Jesus' name. Amen.

My "I AM" Affirmation:
I AM gifted because the Spirit of the living God is within me. I am willing to generously share my gifts because of all that He has given me.

Today, I will:

> ➢ Thank God for giving me special gifts.
> ➢ Thank God for giving me a generous desire to share my gifts with others.
> ➢ Seek the opportunity to encourage someone else.

My thoughts: _____

_____

_____

_____

I AM
Holy
~~ dedicated or devoted to the service of God or the church ~~

"Because it is written, "Be holy, for I am holy.""
I Peter 1:16

I AM
Healed
~~ to make healthy, whole, or sound; restore to health;
free from ailment ~~

"who Himself bore our sins in His own body on the tree, that we, having died to sins, might live for righteousness – by whose stripes you were healed. For you were like sheep going astray, but have now returned to the Shepherd
and Overseer of your souls."
I Peter 2:24 – 25

We are the most complex of God's creations. Created in Him image, but marred by sin, we are the products of both nature and nurture. Somewhere in that mix, the "who" that we were created to be has an influence on the direction we follow to reach our destinies. That is plainly seen in the dynamics of large families. Same mother and father, yet children's lives often take totally different directions based on their personal choices and the impact of outside influences.

The Church is God's large family, and it is filled with many unique individuals. Yet, His plan for our lives, though taking different paths, has only one destination in mind for us all. David declared in Psalm 51:5, "... *I was brought forth in iniquity, and in sin my mother conceived me.*" We were born with a sin nature, but praise God, we were reborn with a holy nature. Jesus Christ, by paying the sin debt that we owed but were unable to pay, healed us from all manner of sickness and disease. It is at our rebirth that we must decide which of these natures we will nurture and develop. We know that whichever one we feed the most is the one which will dominate our lives. As we walk toward our destinies, don't forget that the Lord expects us to be holy, because He is holy.

Holiness, like a coin, has two sides.[14] It is not just what we are. It is also what we do. As soon as we are saved, we are **made** holy. Like the thief on the cross, from the first moment we say "yes", we are holy. We are God's, having been *"bought with a price"*. We are separated from the world. We are consecrated for His purpose. When we are saved, holiness is an imputed (attributed) and immutable (unchangeable) characteristic because God has separated us from the world and made us His own. Purity is the first characteristic of holiness, but that is not all of it.

Holiness is a practice and a lifestyle. You are doing something important and life-changing by feeding the spiritual side of yourself. We are called to holiness, to put it on as a garment, and to conduct ourselves in holiness – in all things. *"… be renewed in the spirit of your mind …put on the new man which was created according to God, in true righteousness and holiness."* (Ephesians 4:23 – 24)

When you start believing God and seeing yourself as holy, your behavior changes because your mind is changed. Your mind is changed as you spend time in the Word, time in prayer, and time practicing life according to the Word of God. It's not so much a matter of holding yourself to a higher standard and it is the idea of doing some things just becomes inconceivable to you. You want to please God! And the more you live in a state of holiness, living before the face of God, the more ridiculous sin seems to you. (You start to wonder why you ever did some of the things you did!!) The change is usually gradual (sort of like losing weight). Often, you

---

[14] Portions excerpted from http://www.pursuingholiness.com/what-is-holiness/

won't see the full extent of the change in yourself. You holiness will be reflected in your healthiness. No more stinking thinking. No more defeated attitudes. No more lascivious behavior. This ongoing sanctification is the pursuit of holiness, and it begins by knowing who God is, who we are, and surrendering to the changes He is making in us.

Prayer of Affirmation ~~
Father, thank You for placing Your Spirit with me, making me holy and healed in You. I thank You that I am healed emotionally, spiritually, and physically. Because the outpouring of Your Spirit upon me has made me new, I declare that I am healed and holy! I will live in my holiness as a badge of honor which reflects Your glory. Please do a work in me to keep me humble and thankful to You for all Your wondrous blessings in my life. Thank You, Lord, for healing me mind, body, and soul, and declaring me holy. In Jesus' name. Amen.

My "I AM" Affirmation:
I AM healed and holy because of the finished work of Jesus Christ.

Today, I will:

- Walk in humble holiness before God.
- Repent immediately for any thoughts or actions which may deflect glory from God.
- Thank God for making healthy in my spirit, mind, and body.
- Seek the opportunity to encourage someone else.

My thoughts: _____

_____

_____

I AM
Intelligent

*~~ having good understanding or a high mental capacity;
quick to comprehend ~~*

"The fear of the Lord is the instruction of wisdom,
and before honor is humility."
Proverbs 15:33

Learning to heed the counsel of others is a sign of maturity. The breadth of our own intelligence is limited to our life's experiences. We need good advice from those whom we trust. Most importantly, we need to follow and walk in the wisdom of God. Walking in obedience to the Lord is the key to our walking in favor, it is the pathway to our living victorious lives in wisdom.

When we learn to keep the Word of God as our counsel, people will look at us in wonder. They will see us walking in the favor of God and not understand it. They will envy us and want to realize the blessings which will be evident in our lives.

If we want to live the God-filled life, it is not enough to know the Word. We must be willing to live the Word. We have to go from giving good advice to walking it out in our own lives. Like good medicine, we have to take it in and allow it work out of us whatever it is that is ailing us.

Prayer of Affirmation ~~
Thank You, Lord, that I am intelligent because I have the mind of Christ working in me. I promise to daily renew my mind and remain focused on the things which You have ordained for my life. I thank You for ordering my steps and making me smart enough to walk that way. Thank You, Lord, for making me an intelligent Woman of God. In Jesus' name. Amen.

My "I AM" Affirmation:
I AM intelligent because I have decided to *"let this mind be in me which was also in Christ Jesus"*.

Today, I will:

- Renew my mind with the Word of God.
- Seek God for the direction to make intelligent choices.
- Allow the Holy Spirit to direct my path in all things.
- Be willing to accept counsel from God-fearing believers.
- Seek the opportunity to encourage someone else.

My thoughts: _____

_____

_____

_____

> God will never direct us to be prideful, arrogant and unforgiving, immoral or slothful or full of fear. We step into these things because we are insensitive to the leadership of the Holy Spirit within us.
> Charles Stanley

I AM
Justified
~~ *declared innocent or guiltless; absolve; acquit* ~~

"Therefore, having been justified by faith, we have peace with God through our Lord Jesus Christ,"
Romans 5:1

I AM
Joy-filled
~~ *filled with the emotion of great delight or happiness caused by something exceptionally good or satisfying; keen pleasure; elation* ~~

"You will show me the path of life; in Your presence is fullness of joy; at Your right hand are pleasures forevermore."
Psalm 16:11

Being justified by faith, we have peace with God. Our conscience can no longer accuse us because it has nothing on which to base the judgment. The slate has been wiped clean! Judgment now decides for the sinner instead of against him. Memory looks back upon past sins, with deep sorrow for the sin, but yet with no dread of any penalty to come, because Christ has paid the debt of His people and received the divine receipt. He finished the work He came to do. Unless God can be so unjust as to demand double payment for one debt, no one for whom Jesus died as a substitute can ever be cast into hell.[15]

We believe that God is just (He has to be!). This belief can frighten us at first. But, when we think it through, it is this same belief that

---

[15] Portions excerpted from Bible Gateway: Charles Spurgeon's Morning and Evening, September 25, 2013.

God is just that becomes the pillar of our confidence and peace! It becomes our joy. It is light along our path which allows us to walk in the newness of life in Christ.

Because God is just, I, a sinner, alone and without a substitute, must be punished. But Jesus stands in my place and is punished for me. Now, because God is just, I, a sinner, standing in Christ, can **never** be punished. God would have to change His nature before one soul, for whom Jesus was a substitute, can ever suffer the punishment of the law. Because of Jesus, we can shout with joy and glorious triumph, *"Who shall lay anything to the charge of God's elect?"* Not God, for He has justified us; not Christ, for He has died for us, *"yea rather has risen again"*.

My joy-filled hope lives not because I am not a sinner, but because I am a sinner for whom Christ died. My trust is not that I am holy, but that being unholy, He has imputed my holiness. My faith rests not upon what I am, or shall be, or feel, or know, but in what Christ is, in what He has done, and in what He is now doing for me. I have been justified by faith! That gives me great joy.

Prayer of Affirmation ~~
Father, thank You that my life is joy-filled because I have been justified by my faith! You have completely pardoned me and rewritten my history in preparation for my destiny. Hallelujah! I Thank You, Lord, for justifying me. In Jesus' name. Amen.

My "I AM" Affirmation:
I AM justified and no longer live under guilt and condemnation of my past. That newness has given me joy which is overflowing in my life.

Today, I will:

- ➢ Walk in the power of my justification.
- ➢ Let the world see that my life is joy-filled and joyful.
- ➢ Praise God for giving me another chance to live in eternal peace with Him.
- ➢ Seek the opportunity to encourage someone else.

My thoughts: _____

_____

_____

_____

~~~~~~~~~~~~~

"Joy is what happens when we allow ourselves to recognize how good things are. Joy is not necessarily what happens when things unfold according to our plans."
Marianne Williamson (*A Woman's Worth*)

I AM
Kind

~~ having, showing, or proceeding from benevolence ~~

"She opens her mouth with wisdom, and on her
tongue is the law of kindness."
Proverbs 31:26

Kindness is the quality of being warmhearted and considerate, humane and sympathetic. It is the tendency to be forgiving. There are few things more refreshing to people than the kindness of other people. Have you noticed it? Someone smiles at you, and you cannot help but to smile back. A person pays you a compliment, and it warms your heart.

When someone offers you unsolicited help, it makes you feel so much better. Kindness is one of those things which you cannot quantify, but it adds much love, joy, and peace to your life. Aesop said, *"No act of kindness, no matter how small, is ever wasted."*

The Lord expects it of us, and that is why He gifted us with this fruit of Spirit. He **gave** us kindness, not for ourselves, but for us to share with others. It should be a part of our love walk. It brings joy not only to the one to whom it is shown, but also to the one who is showing it. It is a win-win, which makes it even more confusing when people are not kind.

The next time you are frustrated or afraid or discouraged or angry or otherwise having a bad day, decide to be kind to someone else on **purpose**. Seek the Lord's help to do what is right because it is right to do. Make a decision to treat someone nice in spite of how you feel. You will be amazed at the effect this will have on them ~~ and on you.

Prayer of Affirmation ~~
Father, thank You for gifting me with the fruit of kindness. I will purposely exercise this gift so that it will grow and become a natural outflow of my interactions with others. I want my kindness to be a beacon of light which draws people in because they are attracted to Your glory in me. Thank You, Lord, for making me kind. In Jesus' name. Amen.

My "I AM" Affirmation:
I AM kind because it is a reflection of the love and compassion of Christ.

Today, I will:

- Extend a random act of kindness to someone with whom I interact.
- Thank God for the opportunity to be a blessing to someone.
- Seek the opportunity to encourage someone else.

My thoughts: _____

_____

_____

_____

I AM
Loved
~~ held in deep affection; cherished ~~

"That Christ may dwell in your hearts through faith; that you,
being rooted and grounded in love, may be able to comprehend with
all the saints what is the width
and length and depth and height – to know the love
of Christ which passes knowledge; that you may
be filled with all the fullness of God."
Ephesians 3:17 – 19

In an interview with Beliefnet Editor David Kuo[16], Rick Warren said, *"I talk to a lot of believers who say, "You know I just don't love God enough." And I say, "No, that isn't your problem. You just don't understand how much He loves you." If you did, you couldn't help but love Him. You were made to be loved by God. God is love. He didn't need us. But He wanted us. And that is the most amazing thing."*

It's not just amazing. That is a beautiful thing! Up to the point that I heard and believed God's love for me, I had accepted that God loved "the world"; John 3:16 told me so. Up to that point, I believed that God had accepted me as His own; John 1:12 was clear on that. But the day that I heard – and believed – that God loved me for me was the day that my life was changed! I couldn't be good enough or righteous enough or faithful enough to make God love me any more than He already did. **God – loves – ME!!!** What an awesome revelation that was (and still is – everyday).

It was one thing to have head knowledge of God's love for me. But it became something totally different when I believed in my heart

---

[16] http://www.beliefnet.com/Faiths/Christianity/2005/10/Rick-Warren-God-Didnt-Need-Us-He-Wanted-Us.aspx#

that He really loves me. Knowing that God loves me puts everything in my life in perspective.

Interestingly, John Wesley said, *"One of the greatest evidences of God's love to those that love Him is, to send them afflictions, with grace to bear them."* His love gives me strength when I am faced with the struggles of life. I am confident that *"no weapon formed against me shall prosper"* because Yahweh loves me. When my finances are stretched and resources are few, I trust that *"my God shall supply all my needs"* because Jehovah-jireh loves me. When I feel alone, I am confident that I have a Comforter who *"will never leave me nor forsake me"* because my Father loves me. When health challenges try to beat me down, I can rest assured that "it is well with my soul" because I know that Jehovah-rapha loves me.

Hallelujah! I know that God loves me. That knowledge is a powerful weapon in my arsenal against Satan. He loves me!

Prayer of Affirmation ~~
Father, thank You for loving me as though I were Your only child! Your loves brings me joy. Your love makes me feel special. You love lifts me up where I belong. And I am especially grateful that nothing can separate me from Your love. Thank You, Lord, for loving me. In Jesus' name. Amen.

My "I AM" Affirmation:
I AM loved by God and nothing can separate me from His love. Nothing!

Today, I will:

- Thank God for loving me!
- Share the love of Christ with others.
- Seek the opportunity to encourage someone else.

My thoughts: _____

_____

_____

_____

~~~~~~~~~~~~~~~~~~~~~~~~~

"BEING DEEPLY LOVED BY SOMEONE GIVES YOU STRENGTH, WHILE LOVING SOMEONE DEEPLY GIVES YOU COURAGE."
Lao Tzu

God's love is your source for both!!

I AM
Mature

~~ fully developed in body or mind, as a person ~~

"Speaking the truth in love, may grow up in all things
into Him who is the head – Christ – from whom the
whole body, joined and knit together by what every
joint supplies, according to the effective working
by which every part does its share, causes growth
of the body for the edifying of itself in love."
Ephesians 4:15 – 16

We are not here by accident, and we are not here to just occupy space. We are here to enlarge the Kingdom, one soul at a time.

When God created you and me, He had a plan. Ask yourself – "am I fulfilling His plan for my life?" "Am I walking into my destiny?" "Am I we living my life with purpose on purpose?" "Am I maturing as a Christian so that I am becoming more like Christ?"

There is so much joy in doing what you were put here to do. So what's holding you up? What's stopping you from doing what you should be doing? What's keeping you from being all you can be? What's preventing you from living your best life now? Whatever it, decided **on purpose** to begin living **with purpose**. Walk into your destiny. Run to your victory. You won't be fulfilled until you do.

Children play; grown folks work. They just have fun while they do it! Live your life God's way; do it on purpose, and get the greatest thrill of your life. There is no joy like knowing that God is pleased with the work you are doing.

Prayer of Affirmation ~~
Father, thank You for helping us to seek, find, and fulfill that thing which You created us to do. We know that our lives are important to You, and we are grateful to be a part of Your master plan. Help us to recognize that we all have a rendezvous with destiny, and let us walk boldly towards it on purpose with purpose. Thank You, Lord, for growing us up in You so that we may become mature Christians prepared to do Your will. In Jesus' name. Amen.

My "I AM" Affirmation:
I AM mature in my thoughts and actions. I am not ruled by my selfish desires but by the power of the Holy Spirit.

Today, I will:

- Look for God at work around me.
- Join God in His work.
- Thank God for entrusting me to work on His behalf as He helps me to mature in Him.
- Seek the opportunity to encourage someone else.

My thoughts: _____

_____

_____

_____

I AM

~~ having been made or come into being only a short time ago; not previously experienced or encountered; novel or unfamiliar ~~

"Therefore, if anyone is in Christ, he is a new creation; old things have passed away; behold, all things have become new."
II Corinthians 5:17

"that you put off, concerning your former conduct, the old man which grows corrupt according to the deceitful lusts, and be renewed in the spirit of your mind, and that you put on the new man which was created according to God, in true righteousness and holiness."
Ephesians 4:22 – 24

There is something about our personalities which just loves new. Decorating a new home. That new-car smell is intoxicating. A new outfit or a new pair of shoes. We love new things.

God has given us the gift of new life which cannot be compared to anything we might acquire on our own. He has renewed us by faith so that we can start anew in our relationship with Him. We have been given a "do-over"! Isn't that just the coolest thing? Born in sin, we received salvation by the grace of God through faith. By faith, we have been given new life, and we don't ever have to look back at what was.

Israel Houghton expresses it well in his song, "Moving Forward". He sings, "I'm not going back, I'm moving ahead. Here to declare to You my past is over. In You, all things are made new, surrendered my life to Christ. I'm moving, moving forward."[17]

---

[17] http://www.metrolyrics.com/moving-forward-lyrics-israel-houghton.html

That should be all of our testimonies. Jesus died so that we could move forward and not look back. He said that anyone who looks back is *"not fit for the Kingdom"*. We are free from the penalty and the power of sin. We have been made holy and righteous. We have been sanctified and are waiting to be glorified. There is nothing in our past worth returning to. Our future is ahead of us.

Why, then, do you think we so easily slip back into our old ways? Everything about our new life in Christ is good. All the Lord asks in return is that we live so that He is honored and His name is glorified. That means changing the way we think. We have to renew our minds. That mean changing the way we talk. We cannot bless God and curse others out of the same mouth. That means not giving in to Satan's temptations. We must focus on the things of God.

God gave us a "do-over"! There aren't many things that offer us second chances. But God has given us new life in Him, and it's better than anything we thought we had the first time. It honors Him when we keep moving forward.

Prayer of Affirmation ~~
Father, thank You for making me new again in You. I have a new walk, a new attitude, a new way of believing, and a new way of living. Give me a heart's desire to emulate You in all areas of my life, renewing my mind daily through Your Word. Help me to develop and nurture the gifts and maximize the opportunities You give to me each day. Thank You, Lord, for making me new. In Jesus' name. Amen.

My "I AM" Affirmation:
I AM a new creation in Christ. Today is filled with exciting possibilities and opportunities to experience the fullness of my new life in Him.

Today, I will:

- ➢ Approach this new day as a fresh opportunity to grow in Christ.
- ➢ Trust God for the experiences which help me to develop in Him.
- ➢ Determine to learn one new thing about the Lord and His plan for my life.
- ➢ Seek the opportunity to encourage someone else.

My thoughts: _____

_____

_____

_____

I AM
Obedient

~~ obeying or willing to obey; complying with or submissive to authority ~~

"If you are willing and obedient, you shall
eat the good of the land;..."
Isaiah 1:19

What a beautiful promise. "If you obey Me, I will..." God only asks for my obedience. In return, He will bless me to enjoy the good things which He provides. By providing me with "the good of the land", God is promising that all my needs will be met.

We limit our blessings by placing all of them in the box of materialism. But God has promised us so much more than that. A life well-lived is not measured by the acquisition of stuff and things. It is a life of contentment and peace, hope and joy. It is a life which appreciates the love of God and freely shares that love with others. It is the life of a person who heard and understood Jesus' statement "if you love Me, you will keep My commandments".

Living in complete obedience to God is so much easier than the way we choose to live our lives. Like Israel, we get caught up in cycles of disobedience, chastisement, repentance, and self-righteousness. Until we reach a point of complete desperation, we will always find ourselves back in that same cycle – disobedience, chastisement, repentance, and self-righteousness. It takes a lot of work to be one way at home, another way at work, and still another way at church. We have to remember which person to take where (hah!) and how that person should behave, depending on who the audience is.
God loves us, and He wants us to love Him in return. Real love seeks to do good. Real love doesn't grieve the person it loves. Real love gives. God is asking us to love Him by obeying Him. The

blessing is ours because He has promised that if we obey Him, we will enjoy "the good of the land".

What a privilege it is to live a life of obedience!

Prayer of Affirmation ~~
Father, thank You for giving me Your written Word for direction and Your living Word for the inspiration I need to obediently follow it. Rather than continuing to walk in darkness, give me the desire to put off deceitfulness and choose to live in the light of Your Word. As I walk in complete obedience to Your Word and in openness before Your people, I want my life to be a living epistle that others can read as I show the world Your glory. Thank You, Lord, for giving me a desire to live in obedience. In Jesus' name. Amen.

My "I AM" Affirmation:
I AM obedient to the Lord, continually seeking His direction for my life.

Today, I will:

- ➤ Seek God for direction for this day.
- ➤ Decide – in advance – that I will be obedient to His direction, without question.
- ➤ Thank God for giving me His Word to help me better understand His direction.
- ➤ Seek the opportunity to encourage someone else.

My thoughts: _____

_____

_____

_____

I AM
Precious in His Sight
*~~ highly esteemed for some spiritual, nonmaterial,
or moral quality ~~*

"She is more precious than rubies, ..."
Proverbs 3:15

"Since you were precious in My sight, you have been honored,
and I have loved you; therefore I will give men for you,
and people for your life. Fear not, for I am with you; ..."
Isaiah 43:4 – 5

God calls us precious. The God of the universe, the creator of heaven and earth, considers us precious. He has called us friend. He loves us with an unrestrained love. He sent His Son to die in our stead. *This God* calls us precious!

If the God who sees all and knows all calls us precious, what more do we need to recognize that we are? God has prepared a special place for us with a particular role for us to fulfill. He has entrusted us to be His hands and feet in the earth, telling the story of the gospel until He comes back. And He has made us a promise to be with us, so we should not be afraid.

To be precious is to be treasured, to be considered special, to be looked upon with favor and delight. Doesn't that just make you feel good to know that God sees you as His treasure, that you are special to Him, and that He looks upon you with favor and delight? In spite of what others say about you, you can know for a certainty that you are all that because God says you are.

So, my precious sister, know how much you are loved and esteemed. Allow that powerful love to lift you up where you belong. You are a citizen of the Kingdom. Isn't it time that you started living like you are? You are precious. Wow!

Prayer of Affirmation ~~
Father, thank You for being the keeper and sustainer of my life who sees me as precious in His sight. Trials come, but it is You who brings me safely through. Thank You, Lord, for Your faithfulness. Thank You, Lord, for Your strength. Thank You, Lord, for Your unfailing love. Because of who You are, I am confident in whom I am, and I am confident that You will see me through because I am more than a conqueror. Thank You, Lord, for calling me precious. In Jesus' name. Amen.

My "I AM" Affirmation:
I AM precious in the sight of God. So, I will honor myself as a special treasure because that is who God says I am.

Today, I will:

- ➢ See myself as God sees me.
- ➢ Consider myself precious without being haughty.
- ➢ Love myself in a healthy way so that I can learn to share that love with others.
- ➢ Seek the opportunity to encourage someone else.

My thoughts: _____

_____

_____

_____

I AM
His Queen

~~ a woman, or something personified as a woman, that is foremost or preeminent in any respect ~~

"But you are a chosen generation, a royal priesthood,
a holy nation, His own special people, that you
may proclaim the praises of Him who called
you out of darkness into His marvelous light;..."
I Peter 2:9 (NKJV)

When we know important people, we want everyone to know that we know important people. We 'casually' mention it to impress others. We feel compelled to let others know about our experience. It makes us feel significant to have people think that we know people in power or position.

Well, we should feel like we are on top of the world! We don't know just an important person; we are hooked up with the most-important people of all times. "The Godhead, three in One – Father, Spirit, Son. The Lion and the Lamb. How great is our God." And He calls us friends!

We are connected to the King of kings. We are not dropping the name of the president of the United States or the Queen of England. It's not Warren Buffet or Beyonce Knowles. It's Jehovah, whose name is above every other name. "The splendor of a King, clothed in majesty. Let all the earth rejoice. How great is our God!"

Do you know Him? Well, He knows you, and He wants you to know Him. There aren't very many dignitaries who want to spend their time with everyone. They feel that they are too important and their time is too valuable. Not so with God! He is never too busy for us. Even though He is the Great "I Am", He wants to have a personal, intimate relationship with each one of us. He has called us His own, making us royalty in His Kingdom. That's something to brag about!

Prayer of Affirmation ~~
Father, thank You that You know us better than we know ourselves. And knowing us, even with our faults and shortcomings, You love us and have called us into relationship with You. That is so amazing, and it is so exciting, because knowing You is the best thing that could ever happen to us. Thank You, Lord, for making us your queens in the earth. In Jesus' name. Amen.

My "I AM" Affirmation:
I AM a queen because I am a part of God's family, a part of His royal priesthood, and I will live with the expectancy of being treated like a part of His royal family.

Today, I will:

> ➤ Praise God for making me an heir in His Kingdom.
> ➤ Live my life in ways which honor Him.
> ➤ Honor myself as I give honor to others.
> ➤ Seek the opportunity to encourage someone else.

My thoughts: _____

_____

_____

_____

I AM
Righteous
~~ *characterized by uprightness or morality* ~~

"For He made Him who knew no sin to be sin for us,
that we might become the righteousness of God in Him."
II Corinthians 5:21

Christians allow themselves to believe Satan's lie that righteousness is unattainable. They make it seem so other-worldly that it is impossible for us as we live day by day. Yet, God expects us to live righteous and holy lives. So the question becomes, how do we do it?

It's simple really – it happens one step at a time. It is a daily walk with the Lord, minute by minute, hour by hour, day by day. We need to approach each new day thanking the Lord for His new mercies and asking for His help in keeping us right with Him. Pray without ceasing. Every step you take, every move you make should be done only after seeking the Lord's guidance.

In this instance, we can rightly say that God knows our hearts. He blesses our intent. Don't be too hard on yourself when you make a mistake. 'Oops! I failed.' Repent, with a heart of contrition, ask the Lord for forgiveness, and ask Him for the added strength to not make that same mistake again. On the other hand, don't allow that mistake be the reason that you continue in sin.

We have been made righteous by the blood of Jesus. We didn't earn it and we don't deserve it, but we've got it. Walking out our holiness and righteousness requires a made-up mind and the continual help of the Holy Spirit. If you want to do it, you can do it, but *only if you want to*. Start watching the little things – what you say and how you say it, your reaction to things people say to you, being honest when tested or tempted to do otherwise. Start making a conscious effort to do what's right in the little things, and soon, your attitude will take on a form of righteousness that you never thought possible. Just try it – you'll like it!

Prayer of Affirmation ~~
Father, thank You that You have made us the righteousness of Christ and given us Your Holy Spirit to lead and guide us in all ways of the truth. Help us to seek You, in all our ways, so that we can become more like You, changing everyday as we "grow up in You" from glory to glory. Thank You, Lord, for imputing righteousness in us. In Jesus' name. Amen.

My "I AM" Affirmation:
I AM righteous because God has declared me righteous. With my head lifted up, I will live as the redeemed righteousness of God.

Today, I will:

- ➤ Declare that I am righteous because of the blood of Jesus.
- ➤ Live in righteousness, seeking God for direction.
- ➤ Thank God for empowering me to live in righteousness everyday.
- ➤ Seek the opportunity to encourage someone else.

My thoughts: _____

_____

_____

_____

I AM
Saved

~~ to rescue from danger or possible harm, injury, or loss ~~

"that if you confess with your mouth the Lord Jesus
and believe in your heart that God has raised Him
from the dead, you will be saved."
Romans 10:9

I AM
Sanctified

~~ made holy; consecrated ~~

"And such were some of you. But you were washed, but you were sanctified, but you were justified in the name of the Lord Jesus and by the Spirit of our God."
I Corinthians 6:11 (NKJV)

Each of the three Divine Persons of the Godhead extends to us their gracious acts. It is just as wrong to magnify the decree of the Father, and the atonement of the Son, and not appreciate the work of the Spirit. In deeds of grace, none of the Persons of the Trinity act apart from the rest. They are as united in their deeds as in their essence.[18]

And as believers and followers of Christ, we must also set a high value on sanctification – upon being set apart to purity of life and godliness of conversation. Sanctified by God the Father. Sanctified by Jesus the Christ. Sanctified by the Holy Spirit. God in three persons, blessed Trinity! We must value the blood of Christ as the foundation of our hope, but never speak disparagingly of the work

---

[18] Portions excerpted from Bible Gateway: Charles Spurgeon's Morning and Evening. July 12, 2013.

of the Spirit which prepares us for the inheritance of the saints in light. From this day forward, let us live so as to manifest the work of the Triune God in us.

We have been saved and sanctified, set apart for His good works. That makes us precious, special, unique, righteousness, and holy. Live that way!

Prayer of Affirmation ~~
Father, thank You for giving us all of You so that we can experience You in all three persons. Thank You for being our loving Father, our Savior Jesus, and our indwelling, sanctifying Spirit. We thank You that we can be assured of our salvation and sanctification in You because You have given us these great gifts. Thank You, Lord, for the love of the blessed Trinity. In Jesus' name. Amen.

My "I AM" Affirmation:
I AM saved and sanctified. Hallelujah!

Today, I will:

- ➢ Praise God for saving and sanctifying me.
- ➢ Live out my day as one who has been sanctified by the blood*.
- ➢ Thank God for His Holy Spirit which helps to live out my sanctification.
- ➢ Seek the opportunity to encourage someone else.

****

* Think about it: what does this mean to you? You should:
- ✓ Guard your mouth – no swearing or lying.
- ✓ Guard your eyes – no lusting or coveting.
- ✓ Guard your hands – no touching the "unclean" things.
- ✓ Guard your feet – don't go anywhere which will dishonor God.
- ✓ Guard your ears – no listening to the "wrong" things, including gossip.

My thoughts: _____

_____

_____

_____

I AM
Thankful
~~ feeling or expressing gratitude; appreciative ~~

"Oh, give thanks to the Lord, for He is good!
For His mercy endures forever."
Psalm 107:1

Bishop Larry Trotter recorded a great song called "Blessing Me". It is also a reminder that we should be thankful for ALL that God is doing for us. *"Every time I turn around, He keeps blessing me. I know I don't deserve it, I've got to run and tell it , how the Lord's been good to me! He keeps blessing me."* I love that song! The words are great, but the beat makes you want to move. Every time I turn around, He keeps blessing me. Every time!! That's why I am thankful to God.

I am continually reminded that God has already done so much for me, carrying me through every situation of my life. It's good to remind ourselves now and again just how much God has done in our lives. He is s-o-o-o-o good, and He is faithful. No matter what our situation may be now, we should be encouraged remembering what He has done. Karl Barth said, *"Joy is the simplest form of gratitude"*. That's what I felt as I listened to that song – joy and real gratitude for all the wonderful blessings that God has given me. Because every time I turn around, He keeps blessing me.

I live under the philosophy that "I can handle what I need to handle, I just need to know what it is that I have to handle". The truth is, I can handle what I need to handle so long as I keep my faith in the One who handles it all. He knows the end of the thing from the beginning, and He is in complete control. My knowing doesn't change anything. It may make me feel empowered, but that's the extent of it. My life is in God's hand. Remembering all that He has done, reminding myself how much He loves me, and never forgetting His faithfulness is all that I really need to know. I can chill out – God's got it! If that doesn't bring joy to your soul, nothing will. Every time I turn around, He's still blessing me!

Prayer of Affirmation ~~
Father, we thank You and praise You for Your goodness and Your faithfulness! We are so grateful to You for all that You do in our lives. Thank You that You care enough to remind us – by any means necessary – that we can always trust You because You do not change. We don't need to know the outcome, just trust You that it will be for our good and for Your glory. Thank You, Lord! In Jesus' name. Amen.

My "I AM" Affirmation:
I AM thankful to God for ALL of His blessings in and on my life.

Today, I will:

- Thank God for this new day.
- Thank God for blessing me.
- Thank God for protecting me and providing for me.
- Seek the opportunity to encourage someone else.

My thoughts: _____

_____

_____

_____

I AM
Unique
~~ having no like or equal; unparalleled; incomparable ~~

"but my dove, my perfect one, is unique,
the only daughter of her mother,
the favorite of the one who bore her.
The young women saw her and called her blessed;
the queens and concubines praised her."
Song of Solomon 6:9 (NIV)

We are all individuals, with unique personalities and outlooks on life. We encounter many things in our lives which may cause us concern.

"For You formed my inward parts; You covered me in my mother's womb. I will praise You, for I am fearfully and wonderfully made; marvelous are Your works, and that my soul knows very well." (Psalm 139:13 – 14 NKJV) I don't know if you know this, but we are all unique and special. Society applauds those traits in people. At the same time, people struggle trying to fit in. Sadly, in the Church, recognizing our unique places in the Kingdom has been likened to arrogance or haughtiness. We **are** somebody special. Add to that our spiritual giftedness and the fact that we are the King's children, and we cannot deny that we are unique and exceptional!

I always knew I was unique, I just had a hard time recognizing what that meant. I was too busy trying to fit it, trying to be what I thought was an acceptable image based on what I saw in others around me. But even when I was bashful and intimidated by others, I felt special. As I grew taller than all my friends, I felt special. When I was made to feel that I was nothing and nobody, I felt special. Then, one day my soul opened up, and I finally got it!

We may not feel that who we are or what we do matters, but we matter to God. His purpose for us, lived out daily as we walk into our destinies, is unique for each of us. And when we are living out our ordained purpose, life is good! We were created **on** purpose **for** a purpose. There is nothing more fulfilling in life than living our lives according to God's plan.

Life is good. Live it! Embrace it! Appreciate it! It is the only one we get, and we owe it to the Lord to live our best lives now. You are unique – be a part of the wonders of each day. And show your gratitude to God by **living** your life.

Prayer of Affirmation ~~
Father, thank You for making me unique! Help us to live out my special differences with excitement, with appreciation, with gratitude to You because You made me this way on purpose with purpose. Open my eyes so that I no longer see differences, but uniqueness, which is to be embraced and celebrated. You died so that I could have lives my life out loud! Help me to walk in the fullness of all that You have prepared. Thank You, Lord, for making me unique. In Jesus' name. Amen.

My "I AM" Affirmation:
I AM unique, which makes me exceptional and special.

Today, I will:

- ➢ Celebrate the unique individuality of being me.
- ➢ Thank God for making me who I am.
- ➢ Embrace my uniqueness as another gift from God.
- ➢ Seek the opportunity to encourage someone else.

My thoughts: _____

_____

_____

_____

"WHY ARE YOU TRYING SO HARD TO FIT IN WHEN YOU WERE BORN TO **STAND OUT**?"
Oprah Winfrey

I AM
Valuable

~~ having qualities worthy of respect, admiration, or esteem ~~

"Do not fear therefore; you are of more value
than many sparrows."
Matthew 10:31

"But we have this treasure in earthen vessels, that the excellence of
the power may be of God and not of us."
II Corinthians 4:7

Have you ever noticed that Rolls Royce and Bentley don't have commercials? Why is that? It's because they know the value their products is what brings customers to them. When you know your value, you don't have to beg people to like you or accept you or believe in you. You can be confident in who you are, recognizing that everyone cannot afford the luxury of being in relationship with you!

As we respect God's majesty, we must compare ourselves to His greatness. When we look at creation, we often feel small by comparison. To feel small is a healthy way to get back to reality, but God does not want us to dwell on our smallness. Humility means proper respect for God, not self-deprecation.

When we look at the vast expanse of creation, we wonder how God could be concerned for people who constantly disappoint him. Yet God created us only a little lower than Himself and the angels! The next time you question your worth as a person, remember that God considers you highly valuable. We have great worth because we bear the stamp of the Creator. A quick read of Genesis 1:26 – 27 will show the extent of worth God places on all people. Because God has already declared how valuable we are to him, we can be set free from feelings of worthlessness.[19]

"He knows how we are formed; He remembers that we are dust" (Psalm 103:14 NIV). God understands that we are fatally flawed creatures, yet deems us immeasurably valuable no matter how beaten down we are by life. In the apostle Paul's day, it was customary to store treasure in clay jars. The common container disguised its contents and didn't draw attention to the treasure within. You and I might not look like much on the outside. We may appear as common as jars of clay, but inside are hidden incredible treasures. Inside these old cracked pots reside the most incredible treasure of all ... the Spirit of the living God. And that makes us valuable!

Louisa May Alcott's book, *"Little Women"*, includes a conversation from Mrs. March to her three girls, Meg, Jo, and Amy. It was really great advice. She told them, "I only care what you think of yourself. If you feel your value lies in being merely decorative, I fear that someday you might find yourself believing that's all you really are. Time erodes all such beauty. But what it cannot diminish is the wonderful workings of your mind – your humor, your kindness, and your moral courage. These are the things I so cherish in you."

Our culture places an ungodly amount of significance on a woman's appearance. It is almost to the point of idolatry. Outward trappings of appearance are not the real you. The real you is the God in you. God sees us as simple jars of clay containing valuable treasure ... and that makes us beautiful to Him.

---

[19] Bible Gateway. God's Story for My Life: *Of Great Worth*. September 25, 2013.

Prayer of Affirmation ~~
Father, thank You that even though I have been battered and bruised by life, I know that I am still valuable to You. Thank You for loving me so much that You sent Your Son, Jesus, to die for my sins. Thank You for making a way for me to have eternal life through Jesus' sacrifice. Thank You for seeing me as Your priceless treasure. Thank You, Lord, for seeing the value in me. In Jesus' name. Amen.

My "I AM" Affirmation:
I AM valuable because God created me with a distinct purpose to fulfill in the execution of His plan.

Today, I will:

- ➤ Seek God for opportunity to walk in purpose.
- ➤ Believe in my purpose and strive to fulfill it.
- ➤ Thank God for making me valuable.
- ➤ Seek the opportunity to encourage someone else.

My thoughts: _____

_____

_____

_____

I AM
Worshipper

*~~ the actions and lifestyle of a person who expresses
reverent love and devotion to God ~~*

"... they do not rest day or night, saying: "Holy, holy, holy, Lord
God Almighty, Who was and is and is to come!"
"You are worthy, O Lord, to receive glory and honor and power; for
You created all things,
and by Your will they exist and were created."
Revelation 4:8, 11

You cannot imagine my joy and excitement when I read that God has, already prepared and waiting for us, golden crowns and our own mansions in heaven! I can see myself walking around heaven as a child of the King, with my own crown to show everyone who I am and whose I am. It is mind-blowing good news. But I want to tell you something else that is really special about our crowns. God did not prepare them for us to show off, but we will receive our crowns so that we can give them back to Him in worship!

That is true of every gift over which He has made us stewards. Our real worship is not in the Sunday morning gathering of the saints. It is in our everyday, Monday – Sunday walking-around lives. It is in our giving. It is in our loving. It is in our appreciation of His glory all around us. We worship God when we submit our will to His, when we recognize Him as the source of everything in our lives, and when we freely give back to Him our time, talents, and tithes with which He has entrusted us.

True worship – the worship which king David experienced – comes from a lifetime of seeking God, looking for Him in every situation and circumstance and occurrence in your life. Real worship is a lifestyle. It is a burning desire to know Him deep down in your spirit. You will find Him, if you search for Him, with your whole heart. And knowing Him, you will want to spend time with Him, continually. We should live to fellowship with Him. A. W. Tozer states that the goal of every Christian should be to "live in a state of unbroken worship".[20] This is only possible when we continually walk with God.

God is so good to us, and He is worthy of our worship and all our praise. If you want a worship experience, one which invokes the presence of God, start looking for Him in every area of your life. He's there, waiting for you.

Hallelujah! We will join with the heavenly hosts and worship at His feet. We get to give back to Him something priceless and precious as a sacrifice in worship. We get to be among the chosen who cry holy, holy, holy, worshipping God day and night along with the angels. And we get to practice it right here in the earth everyday. When we see Jesus – amen! – because we will see Him as He is, in all His infinite glory. What a time of rejoicing that will be!

Prayer of Affirmation ~~
Father, thank You for placing a worshipper's heart in me. I do not fully understand what my heavenly life will be like, but I know it will be glorious because You will be there in all Your glory. Prepare ne now, shape me now, mold me now, transform me now, into the beautiful worshipper I will be as I live forever in Your presence. Give me the desire to grow up into the fullness of the measure of the stature of Christ, in all things. Thank You, Lord, for the worshipper in me. In Jesus' name. Amen.

---

[20] http://www.gotquestions.org/walk-with-God.html#ixzz2fCpw1j6C

My "I AM" Affirmation:
I AM a worshipper because God deserves all my worship. I worship Him because I love Him more than anything.

Today, I will:

- ➢ Worship the Lord in the beauty of holiness.
- ➢ Believe in God's omnipresence and give Him reverence with my life.
- ➢ Praise God for His wondrous acts in and through my life.
- ➢ Seek the opportunity to encourage someone else.

My thoughts: _____

_____

_____

_____

I AM
(e)Xceptional
~~ *unusually excellent; superior* ~~

"Preserve me, O God, for in You I put my trust.
O my soul, you have said to the Lord,
"You are my Lord, my goodness is nothing apart from You."
As for the saints who are on the earth,
"They are the excellent ones, in whom is all my delight."
Psalm 16:1 – 3

We are the product of our experiences. But how we internalize those experiences and allow them to shape us is the result of the choices we make. Many people grow up in happy homes and become happy adults. Others grow in unhappy homes and (you guessed it) become unhappy adults. But the converse is also true. Many defy the pull of their upbringing and become very different individuals than their parents.

Since no one is responsible for their actions, there is a school of thought which attributes the rise in crime and the lack of accountability to the type of upbringing they had. "My parents expected nothing of me, so I don't know how to do anything." "My parents expected everything of me, so I don't know how to do anything." "Nothing I did was ever good enough, so I don't feel that I measure up." Really?!?!

We serve a God of excellence, and He expects the same from us! What should we do with that? Should we wimp out and blame God for making us feel inferior? Or should we set our standards high and strive to achieve them? You can be assured that God is not going to lower His standards so that we can feel accepted. We can go higher, but we have to do our part to make it happen.

Ralph Martson said, "Excellence is not a skill. It is an attitude." Our success (or failure) begins in our minds. In spite of many challenges at the start of my journey, I decided that my end would be better than my beginning. I wanted more than average or mediocrity. I wanted God's best for my life, and I knew that I had to be willing to give Him my best. I decided to renew my mind everyday as I strive for excellence in Him.

God is good. God is love. God is omnipotent. God is omniscient. "O, Lord, our Lord, how excellent is your name in all the earth"[21]. If my Father God is excellent, He expects no less from His daughter. I don't want to disappoint God, so I am striving to be just like Him.

Yep, I miss the mark. Sometimes, I fall down – hard. But I get back up again, and I decide each day that "today will be an excellent day". I know I won't be perfect until Jesus returns. In the meantime, I promised Him that I would keep pressing toward excellence in every area of my life.

Prayer of Affirmation ~~
Father, thank You for being an excellent God. You are my standard for living. I commit to striving each day to live with a spirit of excellence as You change me from glory to glory. Every day, I will "… press toward the mark for the prize of the high calling of God in Christ Jesus".[22] Thank You, Lord, for modeling excellence for me to emulate. In Jesus' name. Amen.

---

[21] Psalm 8:1
[22] Philippians 3:14

My "I AM" Affirmation:

I AM exceptional because God has made me the head and not the tail, I am above and not beneath.

Today, I will:

- ➢ Thank God that He has made me exceptional.
- ➢ Share my exceptional gifts with others.
- ➢ Allow the gift of meekness to rule so that I am not haughty toward others.
- ➢ Seek the opportunity to encourage someone else.

My thoughts: _____

_____

_____

_____

I AM
Yearning for More of Christ
~~ having an earnest or strong desire; longing ~~

"He has made everything beautiful in its time. Also He has put eternity in their hearts, except that no one can find out the work that God does from beginning to end."
Ecclesiastes 3:11

"That I may know Him and the power of
His resurrection, and the fellowship of His sufferings,
being conformed to His death,"
Philippians 3:10

I am a planner **and** a procrastinator. But one plan with on which I do not procrastinate is spending time with God every day. I gotta have Him! **E-v-e-r-y-d-a-y**! He is the first thing on my mind when I awake, and I take that opportunity to spend time in prayer. I study the Word daily, and I pray some more. I meditate upon that Word because I need it to guide me throughout my day. And He is the last thing on my mind when I shut it down, thanking Him for His protection and provision through another day.

I may put off a lot of things, but spending time with the Lord is too important to my spirit and soul for me to put Him off. I want to **know** Him more and more every day. I want to know His voice. I want to bask in His presence. I love Him too much to settle for anything less, and I owe Him even more.

My life has not always been what I dreamed it would be. But in spite of everything that I have experienced in this life, it has been worth it all! Getting to know Jesus, learning of Him, walking daily with Him, living the blessed life, everything that I've been through has been worth it all. Getting to this point in my relationship with

Him, knowing that the best is yet to come, is worth whatever price I had to pay. And, still, I want to **know** Him more and more!

Prayer of Affirmation ~~
*Father, thank You for giving me one more opportunity to get to **know** You. I want to live my life according to Your plan. Today, You have given me one more chance to spend time with You. One more chance to get to know You intimately. One more chance to live. Help me to learn to keep our priorities straight, putting You first above all things in my life. Continue to keep that fire burning within me so that I never grow weary in my efforts to grow into a daughter who looks just like her Daddy. Thank You, Lord, for placing a yearning for You in my heart. In Jesus' name. Amen.*

My "I AM" Affirmation:
I AM in love with God and yearning for more of Him in every way.

Today, I will:
- ➢ Set aside time to spend with God.
- ➢ Pray throughout the day.
- ➢ Meditate on the Word of God.
- ➢ Seek the opportunity to encourage someone else.

My thoughts: _____

_____

_____

_____

I AM
Zealous for the things of God!
~~ *ardently active, devoted, or diligent; full of, characterized by, or due to zeal* ~~

"Do not let your heart envy sinners, but be zealous
for the fear of the Lord all the day;"
Proverbs 23:17

"Blessed are those who hunger and thirst for righteousness,
for they shall be filled."
Matthew 5:6

Have you ever heard or read or saw something which just ignited a fire in you? You couldn't stop thinking about it. It kept coming to mind, over and over, and you knew that it was a message meant just for you.

That's the feeling I remember after reading "The Shack". I read the book some time ago, but each time I remember the story, it stirs so much longing in me, a deep desire to do something to draw me closer to God. It was not written as a how-to manual, giving "seven steps to a closer walk with God" or "ten things to do to get to know God." It was written as a novel – a story – but told in such a way that it unleashed a deep desire in me to get closer to the Lord.

I thank God that He is constantly stirring the embers in my heart to keep the fire burning. Whether through blessings or adversities, a song or the preached Word, He has a way of keeping me hungering and thirsting for Him. No matter how much I learn about Him, there is always so much more to know. He is infinite, so my quest will not end until I "see Him" in the fullness of who He is. Until then, I'll keep chasing after Him, striving to do His will, and giving Him the glory for every victory in my life.

Prayer of Affirmation ~~
Father, thank You for placing a God-sized hole in my heart which only You can fill. My heart's desire is to know You better, and I will seek Your face daily as I strive to do the work You created me to do. Thank You, Lord, for the zealous desire to live my live fully in You. In Jesus' name. Amen.

My "I AM" Affirmation:
I AM zealous for God and the things of God. I will keep striving to know Him in a more excellent way.

Today, I will:

- Seek God's face daily.
- Allow the Spirit of God to stir up the fire in my spirit.
- Praise God for the many ways He keeps the fire burning within me.
- Seek the opportunity to encourage someone else.

My thoughts: _____

_____

_____

_____

Wow, you made it! Think back over the affirmations of faith which we have shared. You are all that God has said you are and the only thing holding you back from walking into your destiny is YOU.

Now it's your turn. What are your "**I AM**" affirmations of faith? What are going to say about **you** as you work to bring forth your beauty from the ashes of your life and become the glorious woman of God you were created to be????

The love of God will lead you from your dark places to your wealthy places of joy, peace, and contentment in every area of your life.

- ✓ God puts a hunger and thirst deep down in us which only He can fill. We can ignore it for a long time.
- ✓ But as we live life, something will eventually drive us in desperation to seek Him for the answers we need and the realization of who we really are *in Him*.
- ✓ It is through the study of the Word of God that we learn that Jesus came to give us abundant life.

~~~~~~~~~~~~~~~~~~~~~~~~~

*Take pride in how far you have come and
have faith in how far you can go.*
Christian Larson

Know this with a certainty:

- ✓ You do not have to conform to anyone's image of who you should be.
- ✓ You do not have to fit into any mold that anyone created for you.
- ✓ You do not have to remain in misery in any area of your life because of fear of what others may say.
- ✓ If you love God more than anything or anyone and learn to love yourself in a healthy way, you **can** live your life according to God's purpose and plan for you.
- ✓ In God's Word, which reveals His will, is where you can discover the keys to abundant living.
- ✓ Walking in God's purpose will bring a joy and peace which you have never before experienced.
- ✓ Trusting in the Lord with all your heart will help you to see the real **YOU** for the first time in your life.
- ✓ Then, you can fulfill all of the "I AM's" that are you.

I'm not competing with anyone.
But I am challenging myself to
be the best me I can be.

NOTES:

Notes:

Notes:

NOTES:

I can't make people *value* me.
All I can do is show them *who* I am, what I
feel, and what I *believe* in.
It's up to them to realize my *worth*.

www.ingramcontent.com/pod-product-compliance
Lightning Source LLC
Chambersburg PA
CBHW071202090426
42736CB00012B/2418